•*Cooking for Today*•

MEXICAN COOKING

·*Cooking for Today*·

MEXICAN COOKING

ROSEMARY WADEY

Produced by Haldane Mason, London
for
Parragon
13 Whiteladies Road
Clifton
Bristol BS8 1PB

ISBN 0-75252-875-0

Printed in Italy

Reprinted in 1998

Acknowledgements
Art Direction: Ron Samuels
Editor: Joanna Swinnerton
Series Design: Pedro & Frances Prá-Lopez/Kingfisher Design
Page Design: F14 Creative Consultants
Photography and styling: Sue Atkinson
Home Economist: Rosemary Wadey

Photographs on pages 6, 20, 32, 44 and 62 reproduced by permission of
ZEFA Picture Library (UK) Ltd.

Note
Cup measurements in this book are for American cups. Tablespoons are assumed to be 15 ml.
Unless otherwise stated, milk is assumed to be full-fat, eggs are standard size 2
and pepper is freshly ground black pepper.

Contents

CHAPTER ONE

Soups & Starters

Most Mexican food has a 'bite' to it because of the liberal use of chillies in one form or another, and soups and starters are no exception. Soups are generally served at all main meals and are usually fairly substantial, being full of beans and vegetables and having a certain zip from the addition of chillies, some variety of chilli sauce or Tabasco. They also make excellent snacks and light meals when served with rustic bread or rolls or, of course, tortillas – the Mexican form of bread that is served with almost everything.

Tortillas are made from either masa harina (a maize flour) or wheat flour, which are similar but offer slight differences in colour, texture and flavour. The wheat tortillas have the advantage of being a little easier to handle.

Typical Mexican starters include dips made with such ingredients as avocados and roasted pumpkin seeds. Small pieces of tortilla or shaped tortillas are either fried or baked and topped with a variety of ingredients including shellfish, cheese, meat and poultry. Eggs, seafood, vegetables and fruit also feature widely. Guacamole makes a splendid starter when served as a dip, though it also features in many of the other recipes as an accompaniment.

Opposite: *A street stall in Oaxaca, in the south of Mexico.*

STEP 1

STEP 2

STEP 3

STEP 4

VEGETABLE & CHICK-PEA (GARBANZO BEAN) SOUP

A good tasty soup full of vegetables, chicken and chick-peas (garbanzo beans), with just a hint of spiciness to serve on any occasion.

SERVES 4–6

3 tbsp olive oil
1 large onion, chopped finely
2–3 garlic cloves, crushed
$^{1}/_{2}$–1 red chilli, deseeded and chopped very
    finely (see page 76)
1 chicken breast (about 150 g/5 oz)
2 celery sticks, chopped finely
175 g/6 oz carrots, grated coarsely
1.25 litres/2$^{1}/_{4}$ pints chicken stock
2 bay leaves
$^{1}/_{2}$ tsp dried oregano
$^{1}/_{4}$ tsp ground cinnamon
salt and pepper
425 g/14 oz can chick-peas (garbanzo
    beans), drained
250 g/8 oz tomatoes, peeled, deseeded and
    chopped
1 tbsp tomato purée (paste)
chopped fresh coriander (cilantro) or
    parsley, to garnish

1 Heat the oil in a large saucepan and fry the onion, garlic and chilli very gently until softened but not coloured.

2 Slice the chicken thickly, add to the pan and continue to cook until it is well sealed all over.

3 Add the celery, carrots, stock, bay leaves, oregano, cinnamon and seasoning. Bring to the boil, then cover and simmer gently for about 20 minutes, or until the chicken is tender.

4 Remove the chicken from the soup and chop it finely, or cut it into narrow strips

5 Return the chicken to the pan with the chick-peas (garbanzo beans), tomatoes and tomato purée (paste) and cover the pan.

6 Simmer for a further 15–20 minutes, then discard the bay leaves, adjust the seasoning and serve very hot sprinkled with coriander (cilantro) or parsley and with warmed tortillas.

DRIED CHICK-PEAS (GARBANZO BEANS)

Dried chick-peas (garbanzo beans) may be used instead of canned. Soak overnight in cold water, then drain and cook in fresh water for about 1 hour until tender.

STEP 2

STEP 4

STEP 6

STEP 6

BEAN SOUP

Beans feature widely in Mexican cooking, and here pinto beans are cooked with a mixture of vegetables to give a spicy soup with an interesting texture. Serve with tortillas or crusty bread.

SERVES 4

175 g/6 oz pinto beans
1.25 litres/2¼ pints water
175–225 g/6–8 oz carrots, chopped finely
1 large onion, chopped finely
2–3 garlic cloves, crushed
½–1 chilli, deseeded and chopped finely (see page 76)
1 litre / 1¾ pints chicken or vegetable stock
2 tomatoes, peeled and chopped finely
2 celery sticks, sliced very thinly
salt and pepper
1 tbsp chopped fresh coriander (cilantro) (optional)

CROUTONS:
3 slices white bread
fat or oil for deep-frying
1–2 garlic cloves, crushed

1 Soak the beans overnight in cold water; drain and place in a pan with the water. Bring to the boil and boil fast for 10 minutes. Cover and simmer for 2 hours, or until the beans are tender and most of the liquid has evaporated.

2 Add the carrots, onion, garlic, chilli and stock, and bring back to the boil. Cover and simmer for a further 30 minutes or so until very tender.

3 Remove half the beans and vegetables with the cooking juices and press through a sieve or purée in a food processor or blender until smooth.

4 Return the bean purée to the saucepan and add the tomatoes and celery to the soup. Simmer for a further 10–15 minutes or until the celery is just tender, adding a little more stock or water if the soup is too thick.

5 Add seasoning to taste and stir in the chopped coriander (cilantro), if using. Serve with the croûtons.

6 To make the croûtons, remove the crusts from the bread and cut into small cubes. Heat the oil with the garlic in a small frying pan and fry the croûtons until golden brown. Drain on paper towels. The croûtons may be made up to 48 hours in advance and stored in an airtight container.

VARIATION

Pinto beans are widely available, but if you cannot find them or you wish to vary the recipe you can use cannellini beans or black-eyed peas as an alternative.

STEP 1

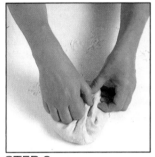

STEP 2

STEP 3

STEP 4

TORTILLAS

Tortillas are eaten with almost everything in Mexico in place of bread. Traditionally, they are made with masa harina (coarse-textured maize meal) but they can also be made with wheat flour. I have found a mixture of maize meal and plain flour also makes an excellent tortilla.

MAKES 10

WHEAT TORTILLAS:
300 g/10 oz plain (all-purpose) white flour
1 tsp salt
60 g/2 oz white vegetable fat (shortening)
150–175 ml/5–6 fl oz warm water

CORN TORTILLAS:
150 g/5 oz plain (all-purpose) white flour
1 tsp salt
150 g/5 oz maize meal
45 g/1½ oz white vegetable fat (shortening)
150–175 ml/5–6 fl oz warm water

1 To make the wheat tortillas, sift the flour and salt into a bowl and rub the fat into the flour with your fingertips until the mixture resembles very fine breadcrumbs.

2 Add sufficient warm water to mix to a softish pliable dough; turn out on to a lightly floured work surface and knead until smooth (2–3 minutes). Place in a plastic bag and leave to rest for about 15 minutes. [Steps 1 and 2 may be done in a food processor.]

3 Divide the dough into 10 equal pieces and keep covered with a damp cloth to prevent it from drying out.

Roll out each piece of dough on a lightly floured work surface to a circle of 18–20 cm/7–8 inches. Place the tortillas between sheets of paper towel as they are made to prevent them from drying out.

4 Heat a griddle or heavy-based frying pan until just beginning to smoke. Brush off all excess flour from each tortilla, place in the pan and cook for 20–30 seconds only on each side until just speckled brown. They will quickly bubble from the heat and should be pressed down lightly with a spatula occasionally during cooking. Take care not to burn or brown them too much. If black deposits appear in the pan, scrape them off; they are excess burnt flour from the tortillas. Do not grease the pan.

5 Wrap the tortillas in a clean tea towel or place between sheets of paper towel when cooked to keep them pliable. When cold, wrap in clingfilm if they are not to be used at once. They will keep in the refrigerator for several days.

6 Corn tortillas are made in a similar way, except the flour and salt is sifted into a bowl, the maize meal is mixed in and then the fat is rubbed in finely; continue as for wheat tortillas.

NACHOS

These are triangles of tortilla, deep-fried until they are crisp and topped with a variety of spicy mixtures and grated cheese to brown either under the grill or in the oven.

STEP 1

MAKES 30

5 tortillas (wheat or corn – see page 12)
oil for frying
1 red (bell) pepper, halved and deseeded
300 g/10 oz jar tomato salsa dip
4 spring onions (scallions), trimmed and
    chopped
4 tomatoes, peeled and chopped
500 g/1 lb can refried beans or 1 quantity
    Refried Beans (see page 22)
175 g/6 oz mature Cheddar cheese, grated
3 tbsp grated Parmesan cheese
chopped fresh coriander (cilantro) to
    garnish

1 Stack the tortillas neatly and cut in half with a sharp knife, and then cut each half into 3 wedges to give 6 nachos from each tortilla.

2 Heat about 2.5 cm/1 inch oil in a large frying pan until just smoking. Fry the pieces of tortilla – a few at a time – until crispy and lightly browned, turning once. Remove and drain on paper towels before transferring to baking sheets.

3 Put the (bell) pepper cut-side downwards into a grill pan and place under a preheated moderate grill

STEP 2

until the skin is charred. Remove and leave to cool slightly. Peel off the skin and then chop the (bell) pepper.

4 Put the chopped (bell) pepper in a bowl with the salsa dip, spring onions (scallions) and tomatoes, and mix together well.

5 Mash the refried beans and spread an even layer over each nacho, then top with the tomato salsa mixture.

6 Sprinkle with the cheeses and place under a preheated moderate grill until the cheese bubbles. Alternatively, place in a preheated oven at 200°C/400°F/Gas Mark 6 for about 10 minutes until the cheese is bubbling. Serve hot or cold sprinkled with chopped coriander (cilantro).

STEP 5

SERVING NACHOS

The choice of toppings for nachos is unlimited and they may be served hot or cold as a starter, a snack or an accompaniment for drinks.

STEP 6

STEP 1

STEP 2

STEP 3

STEP 4

GUACAMOLE

This Mexican avocado dip is served as an accompaniment to many other dishes as well as being enjoyed as a starter, with tacos for scooping it up. The chilli content can be varied to suit your own particular taste by increasing the amount of Tabasco sauce used.

SERVES 4

4–6 spring onions (scallions), trimmed
2 large ripe avocados, quartered, stoned and
  peeled
1 tbsp lime juice
2–3 garlic cloves, crushed
few drops of Tabasco sauce
2–4 tomatoes, peeled, deseeded and chopped
  finely
1–2 tbsp soured cream (optional)
salt and pepper
1 tbsp chopped fresh coriander (cilantro) or
  chives

1 Put the spring onions (scallions) into a food processor and chop finely. Cut the avocado into slices, add to the food processor and work until smooth. Alternatively, chop the onions finely with a knife and mash the avocados and onions together thoroughly with a fork.

2 Add the lime juice, garlic and Tabasco sauce to the avocado mixture and work or mash until smoothly blended. Turn out into a bowl.

3 Stir in the chopped tomatoes and the soured cream, if using, and season the mixture to taste. Then mix in half the chopped fresh coriander (cilantro) or chives.

4 Turn the guacamole into a serving bowl, and if it is not to be used immediately, bury one of the avocado stones in it as this will help it to keep its colour. Cover the guacamole tightly with clingfilm until you are ready to use it, removing the avocado stone at the last minute, and sprinkling with the remaining coriander (cilantro) or chives.

5 Serve as a starter with tacos or tortillas; or serve as an accompaniment to such dishes as Chilli con Carne (see page 58) or Chilli Lamb Chops (see page 54); or use with other ingredients as a topping for tortillas or as part of other recipes.

MASHING AVOCADOS

If you are making guacamole without the aid of a food processor, use very ripe avocados or they will not mash easily to give a creamy texture to the guacamole.

16

STEP 3

STEP 4

STEP 5

STEP 6

TOSTADOS

These small round tortillas are deep-fried and topped with refried beans, shredded lettuce and either a fish or egg mixture. Garnish with tomatoes, olives and a creamy avocado sauce, and serve cold as a delicious starter or light snack.

MAKES 8

¹/₂ quantity Tortillas (wheat or corn – see page 12)
oil for frying
500 g/1 lb can refried beans, mashed or 1 quantity Refried Beans (see page 22)
finely shredded lettuce
200 g/7 oz can prawns (shrimp) or tuna fish in brine, well drained, or 4–6 hard-boiled eggs, grated coarsely
2–3 tsp sweet chilli sauce
¹/₄ tsp ground cumin
5–6 tbsp soured cream
3 tomatoes, sliced
2 small ripe avocados
3–4 spring onions (scallions), trimmed and sliced
1–2 garlic cloves, crushed
1 tbsp lime juice
salt and pepper

TO GARNISH:
 stoned black olives, halved
 fresh coriander (cilantro) or parsley

1 Make up the tortilla recipe and divide into 8 pieces, keeping them covered with a damp cloth. Roll out each piece to a thin circle of about 12 cm/5 inches, on a lightly floured work surface. Cook as for large tortillas.

2 Heat about 2.5 cm/1 inch oil in a large frying pan and when just smoking fry the tortillas, one at a time, for a minute or so until a pale golden brown on each side and just crispy. Drain on paper towels and leave to cool.

3 Mash the refried beans and spread a layer over each tortilla, then sprinkle with shredded lettuce.

4 Combine the drained prawns (shrimp) or tuna fish (mashing if necessary), or eggs, chilli sauce, cumin and soured cream, and place a spoonful to one side of each tortilla on the lettuce; then arrange the tomato slices down the other side.

5 Mash the avocados thoroughly with the spring onions (scallions), garlic and lime juice, or process in a food processor until smooth. Season to taste. Place a spoonful of the avocado sauce on top of the other ingredients.

6 Garnish each with halved and stoned black olives and coriander (cilantro) leaves or parsley sprigs. Serve within an hour of preparing or the tortilla may become soggy and the avocado will lose its colour.

CHAPTER TWO

Vegetables & Salads

The excellent fruit and vegetables that appear in colourful profusion in the Mexican market places can be incorporated into delicious dishes to make vegetarian meals, attractive salads and a range of accompaniments. These dishes use a combination of ingredients that may sound a little unusual but produce wonderful results.

Dried beans form a large part of the Mexican diet and feature in many dishes; one of the most popular beans is the pink pinto bean, although black beans, red kidney beans and chick-peas (garbanzo beans) are popular too. They need long, slow cooking to tenderize and to absorb the rich and spicy flavours that are added, but salt should never be added before they are tender or they may never become really edible. Pre-soaking helps to reduce the cooking time but there is no short cut to producing the best stewed beans – only time. Once cooked they can be cooked again to make Refried Beans, a dish that can be eaten on its own or as an ingredient in many other dishes.

Probably the most popular salad is Tomato Salsa. It has many variations, and each family has its own method of preparation, but however it is served, it includes sliced red tomatoes, mixed with sliced or chopped red onions, chillies and lime juice.

Opposite: *A giant desert cactus thrives in Mexico's arid scrub land.*

STEP 2

STEP 3

STEP 5

STEP 6

BASIC STEWED BEANS

Basic stewed beans are used in a variety of Mexican recipes. The cooking time depends on the type and age of the beans – anything between 1½ and 3 hours. Don't add salt until the beans are tender – it prevents them from softening. Red kidney beans are also good to use in this recipe.

SERVES 4

225 g/8 oz pinto beans or cannellini beans
1 large onion, sliced
2 garlic cloves, crushed
1 litre / 1³⁄₄ pints water
salt
chopped fresh coriander (cilantro) or parsley
    to garnish

BEAN STEW:
1 large onion, sliced
2 garlic cloves, crushed
8 rashers streaky bacon, rinded and diced
2 tbsp oil
425 g/14 oz can chopped tomatoes
1 tsp ground cumin
1 tbsp sweet chilli sauce

REFRIED BEANS:
1 onion, chopped
2 garlic cloves, crushed
2 tbsp oil

1 Soak the beans in cold water overnight; or if time is short, cover the beans with boiling water and leave until cold – about 2 hours.

2 Drain the beans and put into a saucepan with the onion, garlic and water, bring to the boil, cover and simmer gently for 1½ hours. Stir well, add more boiling water if necessary, and simmer, covered, for a further 30–90 minutes, or until the beans are tender.

3 When the beans are tender, add salt to taste (about 1 tsp) and continue to cook, uncovered, for about 15 minutes to allow most of the liquor to evaporate to form a thick sauce.

4 Serve the basic beans hot sprinkled with chopped coriander (cilantro) or parsley; or cool, chill and reheat to serve next day; or use in another dish.

5 To make a bean stew, fry the onion, garlic and bacon for 3–4 minutes in the oil, add the canned tomatoes, the basic beans, cumin and chilli sauce, and bring to the boil. Cover and simmer very gently for 30 minutes. Adjust the seasoning and serve.

6 To make refried beans, fry the onion and garlic in the oil until golden brown. Add a quarter of the basic beans with a little of their liquor and mash. Continue adding and mashing the beans, while simmering gently until thick. Adjust the seasoning and serve hot, or cool and chill for up to 1 week.

STEP 1

STEP 2

STEP 3

STEP 4

TOMATO SALSA

This salad is used extensively in Mexican cooking as anything from a dip to a relish and makes its appearance on the table as an accompaniment to almost any dish.

SERVES 4

4 ripe red tomatoes
1 medium red-skinned onion or 6 spring onions (scallions)
1–2 garlic cloves, crushed (optional)
2 tbsp chopped fresh coriander (cilantro)
½ red or green chilli (optional) (see page 76)
finely grated rind of ½–1 lemon or lime
1–2 tbsp lemon or lime juice
pepper

1 Chop the tomatoes fairly finely and evenly, and put into a bowl. They must be firm and a good strong red colour for the best results, but if preferred, they may be peeled by placing them in boiling water for about 20 seconds and then plunging into cold water. The skins should then slip off easily when they are nicked with a knife.

2 Peel and slice the red onions thinly, or trim the spring onions (scallions) and cut into thin slanting slices; add to the tomatoes with the garlic and coriander (cilantro) and mix lightly.

3 Remove the seeds from the red or green chilli, if using, chop the flesh very finely and add to the salad. Treat the chillies with care; do not touch your eyes or face after handling them until you have washed your hands thoroughly. Chilli juices can burn.

4 Add the lemon or lime rind and juice to the salsa, and mix well. Transfer to a serving bowl and sprinkle with pepper.

VARIATION

If you don't like the distinctive flavour of fresh coriander (cilantro), you can replace it with flat-leaf parsley instead.

STORING

This salad may be covered with clingfilm and stored in the refrigerator for up to 36 hours before use.

MEXICAN RICE

This is a traditional way of cooking rice in Mexico. Onions, garlic, tomatoes, chillies and vegetables are added to the rice and cooked in a chicken or vegetable stock.

STEP 2

SERVES 6

300 g / 10 oz long-grain rice
3 tbsp oil
1 large onion, chopped
½ chilli, deseeded and chopped finely (see page 76)
2 large garlic cloves, crushed
4 tomatoes (about 250 g / 8 oz), peeled and chopped
125 g / 4 oz carrots, peeled and chopped
900 ml / 1½ pints chicken or vegetable stock
125 g / 4 oz frozen peas (optional)
salt and pepper
chopped fresh coriander (cilantro) or parsley to garnish

1 Put the rice in a heatproof bowl, cover with boiling water and leave to rest for 10 minutes; then drain very thoroughly.

2 Heat the oil in a pan, add the rice and fry gently, stirring almost constantly for about 5 minutes, or until just beginning to colour.

3 Add the onion, chilli, garlic, tomatoes and carrots, and continue to cook for a minute or so before adding the stock and bringing to the boil.

4 Stir the rice well, cover the pan and simmer gently for 20 minutes without removing the lid.

5 Stir in the peas, if using, and seasoning; continue to cook, covered, for about 5 minutes, or until all the liquid has been absorbed and the rice is tender.

6 If time allows, leave the covered pan to rest for 5–10 minutes, then fork up the rice and serve sprinkled generously with chopped fresh coriander (cilantro) or parsley.

STEP 3

STEP 5

NOTE

The chilli content of this dish can be increased to give a hotter 'Mexican' taste, but be warned – once it has been added, it cannot be removed!

STEP 6

27

STEP 1

STEP 2

STEP 5

STEP 6

CHRISTMAS SALAD

This colourful salad is served as an accompaniment but could easily be served as a main dish. It incorporates vegetables, fruits and nuts to give a wide variety of flavours and textures. It is usually served around Christmas time in Mexico.

SERVES 4

1 cos (romaine) lettuce
125 g/4 oz cooked beetroot
2 oranges
1 green-skinned dessert (eating) apple
1–2 bananas
1 tbsp lime or lemon juice
1 carrot, peeled
1 pomegranate or paw-paw
60 g/2 oz roasted peanuts or flaked
    almonds, toasted

DRESSING:
1 tbsp lime or lemon juice
finely grated rind of ¼ lime or lemon
    (optional)
1 garlic clove, crushed
4 tbsp light olive oil or sunflower oil
1 tsp sugar
salt and pepper

1 Shred the lettuce and arrange on a flat dish.

2 Peel the beetroot if necessary and cut into dice or small slices; then arrange around the edge of the lettuce.

3 Cut away the peel and pith from the oranges and ease out the segments carefully from between the membranes. Arrange the orange segments over the lettuce.

4 Core and chop the apple and put into a bowl with the sliced bananas. Add the lime or lemon juice and toss, then drain off the excess juice.

5 Cut the carrot into julienne strips or peel off in thin strips, using a potato peeler, add to the apple mixture and spoon over the salad.

6 Cut the pomegranate into quarters and ease out the seeds, or halve the paw-paw, discard the seeds and peel and dice. Sprinkle over the salad with the peanuts or almonds.

7 Whisk all the ingredients together for the dressing and either spoon over the salad or serve in a jug.

ADVANCE PREPARATION

The salad may be prepared up to an hour in advance, but without adding the dressing; cover with clingfilm and chill until required. If left any longer, the beetroot will probably bleed into the other ingredients and spoil the appearance.

STEP 3

STEP 4

STEP 5

STEP 6

MEXICAN SALAD

Cooked new potatoes and blanched cauliflower are combined with carrots, olives, capers and gherkins in a tangy mustard dressing for a salad suitable as an accompaniment or as a main dish.

SERVES 4

500 g/1 lb small new potatoes, scraped
salt
250 g/8 oz small cauliflower florets
1–2 carrots, peeled
3 large gherkins
2–3 spring onions (scallions), trimmed
1–2 tbsp capers
12 pitted black olives
1 iceberg lettuce or other lettuce leaves

DRESSING:
1¹/₂–2 tsp Dijon mustard
1 tsp sugar
2 tbsp olive oil
4 tbsp thick mayonnaise
1 tbsp wine vinegar
salt and pepper

TO GARNISH:
1 ripe avocado
1 tbsp lime or lemon juice

1 Cook the potatoes in salted water until they are just tender; drain, cool and either dice or slice. Cook the cauliflower in boiling salted water for 2 minutes. Drain, rinse in cold water and drain again.

2 Cut the carrots into narrow julienne strips and mix with the potatoes and cauliflower.

3 Cut the gherkins and spring onions (scallions) into slanting slices and add them to the salad together with the capers and black olives.

4 Arrange the lettuce leaves on a plate or in a bowl and spoon the salad over the lettuce.

5 To make the dressing, whisk all the ingredients together until completely emulsified. Drizzle the dressing over the salad.

6 Cut the avocado into quarters, then remove the stone and peel. Cut into slices and dip immediately in the lime or lemon juice. Use to garnish the salad just before serving.

USING DIFFERENT VEGETABLES

This salad is a very versatile one – you can incorporate or substitute a variety of other vegetables according to your own personal preferences.

Light Meals & Snacks

Tortillas are the staple 'bread' of Mexico but they can also be shaped, rolled, cut, fried, layered, baked and prepared in numerous other ways to give the widest possible variety of snacks. They can be served hot and cold, to eat in your fingers or with a fork, and with many flavourings, both savoury and sweet. The words Tacos, Quesadillas, Burritos and Fajitas all evoke wonderful pictures of Mexican life; their spicy flavours, with a touch of Spanish influence here and Indian there, are equally distinctive. Mexico has a hot climate and the food tends to be hot and spicy, but the heat of the food often seems to counteract the heat of the sun.

Tempting snacks such as the ones in this section are sold in market places to Mexicans and visitors alike; they are simple to make, for few Mexican dishes are complicated, just very tasty. Be adventurous and serve them to your family and friends at home.

Opposite: *Fresh tortilla snacks being cooked and sold in a market in Mexico City.*

STEP 1

STEP 2

STEP 4

STEP 5

MEXICAN TACOS

This is one of the classic Mexican dishes that everyone knows. Either prepare your own taco shells or buy them ready-made and fill with refried beans, spicy mince, shredded lettuce and soured cream to serve with tomato salsa and guacamole.

SERVES 4

350 g/12 oz lean minced beef
1 onion, chopped finely
3 garlic cloves, crushed
1 chilli, deseeded and chopped very finely
* (see page 76)*
1 celery stick, chopped finely
1 red (bell) pepper
3 tomatoes, peeled and chopped
1 tbsp tomato purée (paste)
1/2 tsp ground cumin
1/2 tsp ground cinnamon
salt and pepper
1 tbsp vinegar
2 tbsp stock or water
1 tbsp chopped fresh coriander (cilantro)
* (optional)*
oil for frying
4 tortillas (wheat or corn)

TO SERVE:
500 g/1 lb can refried beans
shredded lettuce
4 tbsp soured cream
Guacamole (see page 16)
Tomato Salsa (see page 24)

1 Put the beef into a saucepan with the onion, garlic, chilli and celery, and cook gently, stirring frequently, for about 10 minutes until cooked through.

2 Halve the (bell) pepper, remove the seeds and place in the grill pan, cut-side down. Place under a preheated moderate grill until charred. Cool slightly, then peel off the skin and chop the flesh.

3 Add the (bell) pepper and tomatoes to the beef mixture, followed by the tomato purée (paste), spices, seasoning, vinegar and stock. Simmer for 10 minutes, until tender, and all the liquid has evaporated. Stir in the coriander (cilantro), if using.

4 If making your own taco shells, heat 2.5 cm/1 inch oil in a frying pan and when just smoking, add a tortilla and fry briefly until beginning to colour, folding in half during cooking. Remove quickly and drain on paper towels, placing crumpled paper towels in the centre of the taco so it sets in a shell shape. If using bought taco shells, warm in the oven.

5 Mash the refried beans and put a layer in the base of each taco; then cover with the beef mixture, dividing it equally between each taco. Sprinkle with shredded lettuce and drizzle with soured cream. Serve on warmed plates with guacamole and tomato salsa.

STEP 1

STEP 2

STEP 3

STEP 4

QUESADILLAS

These are an ideal vegetarian dish. A 'lightly hot' flavouring is given to the mixture of cheeses, spring onions and coriander that makes up the filling for these folded tortillas, which are baked in the oven.

SERVES 4

8 tortillas (corn or wheat) – see page 12

FILLING:
175 g/6 oz Feta cheese or white Cheshire cheese
175 g/6 oz Mozzarella cheese
6 tbsp grated Parmesan cheese
6 spring onions (scallions), trimmed and chopped
1–2 garlic cloves, crushed
1 tbsp sweet chilli sauce
1 tbsp chopped fresh coriander (cilantro)
1 cooked potato, grated coarsely
salt and pepper
beaten egg or egg white
oil for brushing

TO SERVE:
shredded lettuce
Tomato Salsa (see page 24)

1 To make the filling, grate the Feta and Mozzarella cheeses coarsely into a bowl and mix in the Parmesan cheese, spring onions (scallions), garlic, sweet chilli sauce, coriander (cilantro), grated potato and seasoning.

2 If the tortillas are too firm to bend in half, dip each one into a pan of gently simmering water until just soft and drain on paper towels.

3 Place about 1½ tbsp of the cheese filling on one side of each tortilla and fold in half. Brush the edges with beaten egg or egg white.

4 Fold over and press the edges together well. Place the quesadillas on lightly greased baking sheets and brush each one with a little oil. Cook in a preheated oven at 190°C/375°F/Gas Mark 5 for 12–15 minutes, or until they are lightly browned.

5 Serve the quesadillas either hot or warm with shredded lettuce and tomato salsa as accompaniments.

ALTERNATIVE FILLINGS

This cheese filling makes Quesadillas an excellent dish for vegetarians, but the filling can equally well be based on fish or meat instead. Eggs are another tasty choice for vegetarians.

PORK TACOS

A different way of serving tacos – here the tortillas are rolled with the spicy pork filling inside and then fried to give a crispy outer shell. They may be served with guacamole, tomato salsa and soured cream, and can also be served cold.

STEP 1

MAKES 8

oil for frying
350 g/12 oz lean minced pork
2 rashers bacon, derinded and chopped
1 onion, chopped very finely
2 garlic cloves, crushed
1 tbsp sweet chilli sauce
1–2 tbsp tomato purée (paste)
½ tsp ground cumin
½ tsp dried oregano
salt and pepper
60 g/2 oz button mushrooms, chopped
2 tbsp stock or water
8 small tortillas (wheat or corn – see page 12), about 15 cm/6 inches
salad leaves to garnish

1 Heat the oil in a saucepan, add the pork, bacon, onion and garlic and cook gently, stirring frequently, for about 10 minutes, until almost cooked.

2 Add the chilli sauce, tomato purée (paste), cumin, oregano and seasoning, and continue to cook for a few minutes more; then add the mushrooms and stock or water and cook for a further 2–3 minutes. Adjust the seasoning and leave to cool.

3 Divide the pork mixture between the tortillas, fold in the ends and roll them up tightly; then secure each with a wooden cocktail stick to prevent them unrolling while cooking.

4 Heat about 2.5 cm/1 inch oil in a large frying pan and when just smoking, add the taco rolls, 2 at a time, and fry until a light golden brown all over, turning in the oil as necessary. Alternatively, they may be cooked in deep fat at 180°C/350°F until a light golden brown.

5 Drain thoroughly on paper towels and remove the cocktail sticks carefully. Keep warm while frying the remaining tacos. Serve with a garnish of salad leaves.

STEP 3

STEP 3

VARIATION

These tacos may be made with fillings based on fish, eggs, vegetables and different types of meat. Experiment to find your own tasty recipe!

STEP 4

BURRITOS

A filling of scrambled eggs, together with a spicy pumpkin seed, herb and yogurt mixture and sliced tomatoes, is rolled into either wheat or corn tortillas. Chopped ham, bacon or fish can be added for variety.

STEP 1

STEP 2

STEP 4

STEP 5

SERVES 4

60 g/2 oz pumpkin seeds, toasted
3–4 spring onions (scallions), trimmed and sliced
1 chilli, deseeded and chopped finely (see page 76)
4 tbsp chopped fresh parsley
1 tbsp chopped fresh coriander (cilantro)
6 tbsp natural yogurt
salt and pepper
4 wheat or corn tortillas (see page 12)
30 g/1 oz butter
4 tbsp milk
1 garlic clove, crushed
6 eggs
60 g/2 oz cooked ham or bacon, chopped, or 125 g/4 oz cooked white or smoked fish, flaked
2 tomatoes, peeled and sliced

TO GARNISH:
shredded lettuce
Tomato Salsa (see page 24)

1 Toast the pumpkin seeds lightly (under a moderate grill or in a heavy-based frying pan with no added fat) and chop finely. Put into a food processor with the spring onions (scallions) and chilli and work until well blended.

2 Add the chopped parsley and coriander (cilantro), followed by the yogurt, and blend until well mixed. Season to taste.

3 Wrap the tortillas in foil and warm in a preheated oven at 180°C/350°F/Gas Mark 4 for a few minutes.

4 Melt the butter in a pan with the milk, garlic and seasoning. Remove from the heat and beat in the eggs. Cook over a gentle heat, stirring, until just scrambled. Stir in the ham, bacon or fish.

5 Lay out the tortillas, spoon the scrambled egg down the centre of each and top with the pumpkin seed mixture followed by the sliced tomatoes.

6 Roll up the tortillas and serve as they are, garnished with the shredded lettuce and tomato salsa.

MICROWAVE HINT

If preferred, the burritos may be reheated before serving for 1 minute in a microwave oven set on Full Power.

STEP 1

STEP 2

STEP 3

STEP 5

CHICKEN FAJITAS

This spicy chicken filling, made up of mixed peppers, chillies and mushrooms and flavoured strongly with lime, is put into folded tortillas and topped with soured cream to serve with tomato salsa. Many other fillings can be used – the possibilities are endless.

SERVES 4

2 red (bell) peppers
2 green (bell) peppers
2 tbsp olive oil
2 onions, chopped
3 garlic cloves, crushed
1 chilli, deseeded and chopped finely (see page 76)
2 boneless chicken breasts (about 350 g/ 12 oz)
60 g/2 oz button mushrooms, sliced
2 tsp freshly chopped coriander (cilantro)
grated rind of ¹/₂ lime
2 tbsp lime juice
salt and pepper
4 wheat or corn tortillas (see page 12)
4–6 tbsp soured cream

TO GARNISH:
Tomato Salsa (see page 24)
lime wedges

1 Halve the (bell) peppers, remove the seeds and place skin-side upwards under a preheated moderate grill until well charred. Leave to cool slightly and then peel off the skin; cut the flesh into thin slices.

2 Heat the oil in a pan, add the onions, garlic and chilli, and fry them for a few minutes just until the onion has softened.

3 Cut the chicken into narrow strips, add to the vegetable mixture in the pan and fry for 4–5 minutes until almost cooked through, stirring occasionally.

4 Add the peppers, mushrooms, coriander, lime rind and juice, and continue to cook for 2–3 minutes. Season to taste.

5 Heat the tortillas, wrapped in foil, in a preheated oven at 180°C/350°F/ Gas Mark 4 for a few minutes. Bend them in half and divide the chicken mixture between them.

6 Top the chicken filling in each tortilla with a spoonful of soured cream and serve garnished with tomato salsa and lime wedges.

SEAFOOD ALTERNATIVE

Instead of chicken, 250–300 g/8–10 oz peeled prawns (shrimp) or tiger prawns (jumbo shrimp) may be used.

CHAPTER FOUR

Main Dishes

Fish and shellfish abound both in the bustling seafood markets of Mexico, and all along the coastline where the local fishermen sell their morning catch directly from their boats. Invariably, the seafood is cooked by the simplest of methods, often just with lime juice and with fresh vegetables, spices and herbs, whether it is to be eaten at home with the family or in a restaurant. One speciality called ceviche, consisting of raw fillets of fish or shellfish, is very easy to prepare as it is simply marinated liberally in lime juice, which gives it the appearance and taste of being cooked.

Chicken appears frequently on the menu, while turkey, duck and game are often served on special occasions. All poultry and game dishes are cooked with robust flavourings of spices and herbs, and often incorporate fresh vegetables and fruits, which add to both the taste and texture.

All types of meat feature extensively in Mexican main dishes and appear in many guises, all with a deep, rich flavour. The sauces for all meat dishes tend to be fairly hot and spicy, usually with a liberal addition of fresh or dried chilli or some type of chilli sauce, but of course this can be adapted to suit your own particular taste – simply cut down on the amount of chilli used in the recipe to give a milder but still spicy sauce.

Opposite: *The beach at Acapulco. Fish are plentiful off Mexico's coasts and are used in a variety of tasty dishes.*

STEP 1

STEP 2

STEP 3

STEP 4

PRAWNS (SHRIMP) IN BACON WITH SOURED CREAM

King or tiger prawns (jumbo shrimp) make a splendid meal, especially when wrapped in bacon, grilled with a garlic and lime butter, and served with a spicy and tangy soured cream and coriander (cilantro) sauce.

SERVES 4

16–20 king prawns or large tiger prawns
  (jumbo shrimp)
16–20 lean rashers streaky bacon, derinded
60 g/2 oz butter
finely grated rind of 1 lime
2 garlic cloves, crushed

CORIANDER (CILANTRO) AND SOURED
  CREAM SAUCE:
150 ml/¼ pint soured cream
2–3 garlic cloves, crushed
½ small red chilli, deseeded and chopped
  very finely (see page 76)
2 tbsp chopped fresh coriander (cilantro)
2 spring onions (scallions), trimmed and
  chopped finely
salt and pepper
1–2 tsp lime juice

TO GARNISH:
fresh coriander (cilantro)
lime wedges

1 Remove the heads and shells from the prawns (shrimp) but leave the tails in place. Remove the black vein which runs down the length of the prawn (shrimp).

2 Wrap a rasher of bacon around each prawn (shrimp), securing with a piece of wooden cocktail stick. Place on a foil-lined grill pan.

3 Melt the butter and mix in half the grated lime rind and the garlic. Use to brush over the bacon-wrapped prawns (shrimp).

4 To make the sauce, put the soured cream into a bowl and mix in the garlic, chilli, coriander (cilantro), spring onions (scallions), remaining grated lime rind, seasoning and finally lime juice to taste, which will thicken up the sauce. Transfer to a serving bowl.

5 Cook the prawns (shrimp) under a preheated grill for about 2 minutes on each side, or until the bacon is lightly browned and the prawns (shrimp) are hot. Remove and discard the wooden cocktail sticks.

6 Serve the prawns (shrimp) on a large plate or 4 individual plates, together with the soured cream sauce and a garnish of fresh coriander (cilantro) and lime wedges.

YUCATAN FISH

Herbs, onion, green (bell) pepper and pumpkin seeds are used to flavour this baked fish dish, which is first marinated in lime juice.

STEP 1

STEP 2

STEP 4

STEP 5

SERVES 4

4 cod cutlets or steaks or hake cutlets (about
    175 g/6 oz each)
2 tbsp lime juice
salt and pepper
1 green (bell) pepper
1 tbsp olive oil
1 onion, chopped finely
1–2 garlic cloves, crushed
45 g/1½ oz green pumpkin seeds
grated rind of ½ lime
1 tbsp fresh coriander (cilantro) or parsley,
    chopped
1 tbsp fresh mixed herbs, chopped
60g/2oz button mushrooms, sliced thinly
2–3 tbsp fresh orange juice or white wine

TO GARNISH:
lime wedges
fresh mixed herbs

1 Wipe the fish, place in a shallow ovenproof dish and pour the lime juice over. Turn the fish in the juice, season with salt and pepper, cover and leave in a cool place for 15–30 minutes.

2 Halve the (bell) pepper, remove the seeds and place under a preheated moderate grill, skin-side upwards, until the skin burns and splits. Leave to cool

slightly, then peel off the skin and chop the flesh.

3 Heat the oil in a pan and fry the onion, garlic, (bell) pepper and pumpkin seeds gently for a few minutes until the onion is soft.

4 Stir in the lime rind, coriander (cilantro) or parsley, mixed herbs, mushrooms and seasoning, and spoon over the fish.

5 Spoon or pour the orange juice or wine over the fish, cover with foil or a lid and place in a preheated oven at 180°C/350°F/Gas Mark 4 for about 30 minutes, or until the fish is just tender.

6 Garnish the fish with lime wedges and fresh herbs and serve with Mexican Rice (see page 27) or plain boiled rice and tortillas.

MICROWAVE NOTE

This dish may also be covered with clingfilm and cooked in a microwave oven at Full Power for about 4 minutes.

ENCHILADA LAYERS

The filling for these can be varied considerably by using beef, fish or shellfish. If preferred, the tortillas can be rolled up once they are filled, and baked in the sauce in rolls rather than in layers.

STEP 1

STEP 2

STEP 5

STEP 5

SERVES 4

CHICKEN FILLING:
500 g/1 lb boneless chicken breasts
2 tbsp olive oil
1 large onion, sliced thinly
3 garlic cloves, crushed
1 tsp ground cumin
2 tbsp stock or water
salt and pepper
1 tbsp chopped fresh coriander (cilantro)
chopped fresh coriander (cilantro) to garnish

TOMATO SAUCE:
2 tbsp oil
1 onion, chopped very finely
3 garlic cloves, crushed
1 red chilli, deseeded and chopped finely (see page 76)
425 g/14 oz can chopped tomatoes with herbs
250 g/8 oz can peeled tomatoes, chopped
3 tbsp tomato purée (paste)
2 tbsp lime juice
2 tsp caster (superfine) sugar
salt and pepper
6 tortillas (wheat or corn – see page 12)
175 g/6 oz Feta or white Cheshire cheese, coarsely grated

1 Remove the skin from the chicken and chop the flesh finely. Heat the oil in a pan and fry the onion and garlic gently until soft.

2 Add the chicken and fry for about 5 minutes, or until well sealed and almost cooked, stirring frequently. Add the cumin, stock or water and seasoning, and continue to cook for 2–3 minutes until tender; then stir in the coriander (cilantro) and remove from the heat.

3 To make the tomato sauce, heat the oil in a pan and fry the onion, garlic and chilli gently until softened.

4 Add both cans of tomatoes, the tomato purée (paste), lime juice, sugar and seasoning. Bring to the boil and simmer gently for 10 minutes.

5 Place 1 tortilla on a greased ovenproof dish, cover with a fifth of the chicken mixture and 2 tbsp tomato sauce and sprinkle with cheese. Continue to layer in this way, finishing with a tortilla, the remaining sauce and cheese.

6 Place, uncovered, in a preheated oven at 190°C/375°F/Gas Mark 5 for about 25 minutes, or until lightly browned. Serve cut into wedges and sprinkle with coriander (cilantro).

STEP 1

STEP 2

STEP 3

STEP 3

PICADILLO

This spicy meat hash can be made with beef or with a mixture of beef and pork. It is flavoured with plenty of spices, chilli, raisins and almonds, and may be used as it is, or as a filling for tortillas (see page 12), burritos (see page 40), enchiladas (see page 51), taco shells (see page 34) or chimichangas (see page 66).

SERVES 4

350 g/12 oz lean minced beef
225 g/8 oz minced pork (or beef)
2 onions, sliced thinly
3 garlic cloves, crushed
1 large carrot, chopped finely
1 green chilli, deseeded and chopped finely
   (see page 76)
425 g/14 oz can tomatoes
2 tbsp tomato purée (paste)
90 g/3 oz raisins
150 ml /¼ pint red wine
1 tbsp vinegar
1 tsp cumin
½ tsp ground allspice
½ tsp ground cinnamon
60 g/2 oz blanched flaked almonds
salt and pepper
chopped fresh coriander (cilantro) to garnish

1 Put the meats into a heavy-based saucepan with no extra fat and cook over a low heat until well sealed, stirring frequently.

2 Add the onions, garlic, carrot and chilli to the pan and continue to cook for 3–4 minutes, or until they have softened. Drain off any excess fat.

3 Add the tomatoes, tomato purée (paste), raisins, wine, vinegar, cumin, allspice, cinnamon, half the almonds and seasoning. Stir into the meat and onion mixture.

4 Bring to the boil, cover the pan and simmer gently, stirring occasionally, for 20–30 minutes, or until the meat is tender and most of the liquid has evaporated.

5 Adjust the seasoning to taste and serve the picadillo sprinkled with the remaining almonds and chopped coriander (cilantro).

STUFFING FOR VEGETABLES

This versatile recipe is excellent when topped with a layer of creamed potatoes. Alternatively, it can be used as a stuffing for peppers, courgettes, aubergines (eggplants) and other vegetables.

STEP 1

STEP 3

STEP 5

STEP 6

CHILLI LAMB CHOPS

Leg lamb chops cut straight across the leg joint make a very tender and tasty meal when they are given the Mexican flavouring of chilli, onion, spices and lime.

SERVES 4

4 large lamb leg chops (about 175 g/6 oz
  each)
150 ml /¼ pint red wine
3 large garlic cloves, crushed
½ small onion, chopped
1 small chilli, deseeded and chopped finely
  (see page 76)
2 small thin slices fresh root ginger, chopped
1 tbsp paprika
1½ tsp ground cumin
½ tsp salt
pepper
grated rind of ½ lime
2 tbsp lime juice
oil for frying

TO GARNISH:
lime slices, twisted
2 spring onions (scallions), trimmed and
  sliced
chopped fresh coriander (cilantro) or
  coriander (cilantro) leaves

1 Cover the chops with clingfilm and beat out a little thinner with a meat cleaver or rolling pin.

2 Put the wine into a food processor or blender with the garlic, onion, chilli, ginger, paprika, cumin, salt, pepper, and lime rind and juice. and work until smooth. Alternatively, chop the onion, chilli and garlic very finely by hand and mix well with the other ingredients.

3 Pour a thin layer of the sauce into a container that is just large enough to hold the lamb chops in a single layer, add the chops and cover with the remaining sauce.

4 Cover the lamb with clingfilm and leave in a cool place to marinate for at least 2 hours, preferably 3–4 hours.

5 Heat the oil in a pan. Drain the pieces of lamb and fry each one gently for 3–4 minutes on each side until browned and just cooked through. Pour off any excess fat from the pan, then add the remaining marinade to the pan and cook for 3–4 minutes. Adjust the seasoning to taste.

6 Serve the lamb chops on a platter with the sauce spooned over and garnished with twisted lime slices, sliced spring onions (scallions) and chopped fresh coriander (cilantro) or coriander (cilantro) leaves. Serve with fried or boiled potatoes, tortillas and a salad.

SPICED PORK RIBS WITH APRICOTS

American-style ribs of pork are baked with a selection of spices and then, halfway through cooking, a spicy apricot and onion sauce is added to produce a thick and delicious coating to the pork.

STEP 1

SERVES 4

1.75–2 kg/3¹/₂–4 lb American-style pork
 ribs
salt
1 tbsp coarsely ground black pepper
1 tbsp ground cumin
4 garlic cloves, crushed
2 tbsp chopped fresh coriander (cilantro)
1 tsp ground coriander
1 tbsp oil
chopped fresh coriander (cilantro) to garnish
 (optional)

APRICOT SAUCE:
450 ml/³/₄ pint chicken or beef stock
175 g/6 oz ready-to-eat dried apricot halves
4 garlic cloves, crushed
1 tbsp hot chilli sauce or ¹/₂–1 tsp chilli
 powder
2 tbsp oil
1 large onion, chopped

1 Cut the pork into 5 cm/2 inch pieces and place in an ovenproof dish or tin in a single layer. Season with salt and pepper. Combine the cumin, garlic, fresh coriander (cilantro) and ground coriander, and sprinkle over the pork, rubbing in and turning the pieces so they are evenly coated. Leave to marinate for at least 2 hours.

2 Drizzle the oil over the pork and place in a preheated oven at 200°C/400°F/Gas Mark 6 for 45 minutes, or until lightly browned.

3 Prepare the sauce. Put the stock, apricots, garlic and chilli sauce or powder into a food processor or blender and work until puréed, or chop finely.

STEP 3

4 Heat the 2 tbsp oil and fry the onion until softened but only lightly coloured. Add the apricot purée, bring to the boil and simmer gently for 10 minutes. (If necessary add a little hot water, but the sauce should be thick.)

5 Drain off any excess fat from the pork, then pour the apricot sauce over the ribs and return to the oven for about 20 minutes, or until well browned. Serve hot sprinkled with chopped coriander (cilantro), if liked, and with a salad as an accompaniment.

STEP 4

COOKING OPTION

Alternatively, fry the pork in shallow fat until well browned and cooked through, then serve with the sauce spooned over.

STEP 5

CHILLI CON CARNE

Probably the best-known Mexican dish and one that is a great favourite with all. The chilli content can be increased to suit your taste.

STEP 1

STEP 2

STEP 3

STEP 4

SERVES 4

750 g/1½ lb braising or best stewing steak
2 tbsp oil
1 large onion, sliced
2–4 garlic cloves, crushed
1 tbsp plain (all-purpose) flour
450 ml/¾ pint tomato juice
425 g/14 oz can tomatoes
1–2 tbsp sweet chilli sauce
1 tsp ground cumin
salt and pepper
425 g/14 oz can red kidney beans, drained
½ teaspoon dried oregano
1–2 tbsp chopped fresh parsley
chopped fresh herbs to garnish

1 Cut the beef into cubes of about 2 cm/¾ inch. Heat the oil in a flameproof casserole and fry the beef until well sealed all over. Remove from the casserole.

2 Add the onion and garlic to the casserole and fry in the same oil until lightly browned; then stir in the flour and cook for 1–2 minutes.

3 Stir in the tomato juice and tomatoes gradually and bring to the boil. Replace the beef and add the chilli sauce, cumin and seasoning. Cover

and place in a preheated oven at 160°C/325°F/Gas Mark 3 for 1½ hours, or until almost tender.

4 Stir in the kidney beans, oregano and parsley, and adjust the seasoning to taste. Cover the casserole and return to the oven for 45 minutes, or until the meat is very tender and the sauce is fairly thick.

5 Serve the chilli con carne sprinkled with chopped fresh herbs and with boiled rice and tortillas.

MINCED BEEF

This dish can be made with minced beef, though cubed beef is traditionally used.

ECONOMY HINT

Because chilli con carne requires quite a lengthy cooking time, it saves time and fuel to prepare double the quantity you need and freeze half of it to serve on another occasion. Defrost and use within 3–4 weeks.

CHILLI MEATBALLS

Meatballs are a great favourite and here both the meat and the tomato sauce are spiced, but the result is not too hot. By roasting the pepper and peeling off the skin, any bitterness is removed.

STEP 1

STEP 2

STEP 3

STEP 4

SERVES 4

750 g/1¹/₂ lb minced beef
1 small onion, chopped finely
30 g/1 oz ground almonds
60 g/2 oz fresh white breadcrumbs
1 tsp ground cumin
¹/₄ tsp mild chilli powder
1 tsp freshly chopped thyme or ¹/₂ tsp dried
    thyme
salt and pepper
1 egg, beaten
3–4 tbsp oil for frying
sprigs of fresh thyme or parsley to garnish

SAUCE:
1 onion, sliced
250 g/8 oz tomatoes, peeled
2 garlic cloves, crushed
300 ml /1¹/₂ pint tomato juice
¹/₂–1 red chilli, deseeded and chopped finely
    (see page 76)
1 tsp sweet chilli sauce
1 red pepper

1 To make the meatballs, combine the beef, onion, ground almonds, breadcrumbs, cumin, chilli powder, herbs and seasoning, and bind together with the beaten egg.

2 Divide into 16–20 pieces and shape into round balls.

3 Heat the oil in a pan and fry the meatballs until lightly browned; transfer to a casserole.

4 Purée the onion, tomatoes and garlic in a food processor or blender or chop finely and mix well; pour into a saucepan with the tomato juice, chilli, chilli sauce and seasoning. Bring to the boil and simmer gently for 10 minutes.

5 Cut the pepper in half, remove the seeds and place under a preheated moderate grill, skin-side upwards, and cook until the skin chars. Leave to cool slightly, then peel off the skin and cut the pepper into strips.

6 Add the pepper to the sauce and pour over the meatballs. Cover the casserole and place in a preheated oven at 160°C/325°F/Gas Mark 3 for 30–40 minutes.

7 Adjust the seasoning and serve garnished with thyme or parsley. Serve with rice or potatoes and a salad.

CHAPTER FIVE

Desserts & Cakes

Many tropical fruits grow abundantly in Mexico, including pineapples, guavas, mangoes, passion-fruit, coconuts and all the citrus fruits, and these are used in many of the desserts that are served. Mexicans also love the fried pastries, fritters and pieces of tortilla which are tossed in a spicy sugar mixture after they are fried, and served hot or cold as a dessert or sweet snack.

Every country serves some type of ice cream and Mexico is no exception. Probably the favourite is either a vanilla ice cream with undertones of cinnamon and spices – delicious served alone or with fresh fruits – or a citrus ice cream made by simply adding the finely grated lime, orange or lemon rind to the mixture.

The Mexican version of Bread Pudding is fairly unusual but is certainly one that will quickly become a favourite. The bread is soaked in a spicy sugar syrup, together with raisins, nuts and a thick grating of Cheddar cheese, and then everything is wrapped in tortillas before baking – it is just as good cold as hot.

Yeasted buns and cakes are also popular, often with raisins and nuts added and always spiced in some way; these, along with other cakes and breads, and biscuits, appear in various forms, often made to be served at the religious festivals held throughout the year.

Opposite: *The old Mayan Temple of the Dwarf at Uxmal, Yucatan.*

STEP 1

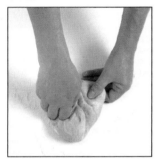

STEP 3

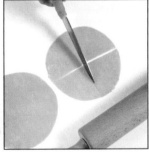

STEP 4

STEP 5

SWEET TORTILLA FRITTERS

Sweet tortillas are cut into triangles to be fried and are served dipped in cinnamon sugar as teatime treats, or with fresh fruits and cream or yogurt for a dessert.

SERVES 4–6

2 eggs
45 g/1¹/₂ oz caster (superfine) sugar
125 g/4 oz plain (all-purpose) flour
90 g/3 oz self-raising flour
pinch of salt
¹/₄ tsp ground cinnamon
oil for shallow frying

CINNAMON SUGAR:
90 g/3 oz caster (superfine) sugar
¹/₂ tsp ground cinnamon
good pinch of ground ginger

TO DECORATE:
clear honey (optional)
mixed fresh fruits

1 Put the eggs and sugar into a bowl and whisk together until very thick and pale in colour, with the whisk leaving a distinct trail. It is best to use an electric hand mixer if you have one.

2 Sift the two flours together with the salt and ground cinnamon. Whisk half of the flour gradually into the egg mixture, then work in the remainder to make a dough.

3 Turn the dough out on a lightly floured work surface and knead until smooth and no longer sticky. (This may be done in a large electric mixer fitted with a dough hook.) Wrap in clingfilm and leave to rest for about 30 minutes.

4 Divide the dough into 6 and roll each piece out to a thin circle of about 20 cm/8 inches; then cut each circle into quarters.

5 Heat about 2.5 cm/1 inch of oil in a pan until a cube of bread will brown in about 1 minute. Fry the fritters, a few at a time, for about 1 minute on each side, until golden brown and bubbly. Drain on paper towels and toss quickly in a mixture of the sugar, cinnamon and ginger.

6 Serve the fritters (hot or cold) on a plate, and, if liked, drizzle a little clear honey over them. Decorate with fresh fruits such as sliced mango, figs, passion-fruit, nectarines, strawberries, guavas and pomegranates, etc.

FRUIT CHIMICHANGAS

Wheat tortillas are folded into quarters with a filling of fruits such as paw-paw, apricot or mango, mixed with orange rind and orange segments and flavoured with cinnamon and sugar, then fried in butter to make a truly delicious dessert.

STEP 1

STEP 2

STEP 3

STEP 3

SERVES 4

1 large paw-paw, or 4 apricots, or 1 large mango
8–12 strawberries
1 large orange
2 tbsp caster (superfine) sugar
¼ tsp ground cinnamon
4 wheat tortillas (see page 12)
60 g/2 oz butter
sifted icing (confectioners') sugar
30 g/1 oz flaked almonds (optional)

1 Halve the paw-paw, scoop out the seeds, peel and cut into small dice; or stone and slice the apricots; or peel the mango, remove the stone and dice the flesh. Slice the strawberries. Put the fruit into a bowl.

2 Finely grate half the rind from the orange and add to the fruit. Cut away the peel and pith from the orange and ease out the segments from between the membranes. Cut the segments in half and mix with the fruit, adding the sugar and cinnamon.

3 Divide the mixture between the tortillas, placing on one side; then fold in half, and in half again to make a quarter or pocket.

4 Melt half the butter in a small pan and fry the chimichangas 2 at a time for 1–2 minutes on each side until golden brown, turning them over carefully. Place on warmed plates, then add the remaining butter to the pan and fry the other 2 chimichangas in the same way.

5 Sift icing (confectioners') sugar over the chimichangas and sprinkle them with the toasted almonds, if using. Serve hot.

OTHER FRUITS

Other fruits such as cherries, strawberries and raspberries can be used for this recipe instead of the tropical fruits.

MEXICAN BREAD PUDDING

This is somewhat different from the bread pudding we know, though it still contains raisins, nuts, orange rind and spices, together with toasted French bread soaked in a syrup, and a layer of mature cheese. The whole mixture is encased and baked in tortillas.

STEP 3

SERVES 6

1 small French stick loaf
60 g/2 oz butter

SYRUP:
175 g/6 oz soft brown sugar
200 ml/7 fl oz water
1 cinnamon stick
6 whole cloves or a pinch of ground cloves
1/4 tsp mixed (apple pie) spice
300 ml/1/2 pint milk
3–4 wheat or corn tortillas (18–20. cm/7–8 inch) (see page 12)
175 g/6 oz raisins
90 g/3 oz almonds, flaked or chopped
grated rind of 1 orange
75 g/2 1/2 oz mature (sharp) Cheddar cheese, grated

1 Cut the French bread into 1 cm/ 1/2 inch slices (about 14) and spread each side lightly with some of the butter. Place on a baking sheet and cook in a preheated oven at 180°C/350°F/Gas Mark 4 for about 10 minutes, or until golden brown.

2 Meanwhile make the syrup: put the sugar and water into a saucepan with the cinnamon stick, cloves and mixed (apple pie) spice. Heat gently until

dissolved and then simmer for 2 minutes. Strain into a jug, discarding the spices, and mix in the milk.

3 Use the remaining butter to grease an ovenproof dish of about 1.7 litre/3 pint capacity. Use the tortillas to line the dish, cutting them to fit neatly.

STEP 4

4 Dip half the baked bread slices into the syrup and lay over the tortillas.

5 Combine the raisins, almonds and orange rind and sprinkle half over the bread, followed by half the cheese.

6 Dip the remaining bread in the syrup and lay over the raisin mixture; then sprinkle with the remaining raisins, nuts, orange rind and cheese.

STEP 5

7 Pour the remaining syrup into the dish, and place in a preheated oven at 200°C/400°F/Gas Mark 6 for 20 minutes. Reduce the temperature to 160°C/325°F/Gas Mark 3, cover with a sheet of greaseproof paper or foil and continue to cook for about 30 minutes. Serve hot, warm or cold cut into wedges, with cream, ice cream or natural yogurt.

STEP 6

CINNAMON BAKED CUSTARD

This dish, similar to the familiar crème caramel, is called a flan in Mexico, and is made either in individual pots or in one large container to be turned out before eating. Serve plain or with cream.

STEP 1

STEP 2

STEP 3

STEP 4

SERVES 6

175 g/6 oz caster (superfine) sugar
3 tbsp water

CUSTARD:
5 eggs
45 g/1½ oz caster (superfine) sugar
600 ml/1 pint milk
3 tbsp double (heavy) cream
few drops of vanilla flavouring (extract)
good pinch of ground allspice
½ tsp ground cinnamon
pouring or whipped cream to serve
   (optional)

1 Prepare a 15–18 cm/6–7 inch deep round cake tin or 6 individual ramekin dishes or dariole moulds by rinsing with cold water. Put the sugar into a heavy-based saucepan with the water and mix together. Heat gently, stirring constantly until the sugar has dissolved. Bring to the boil, increase the heat and boil, uncovered and without further stirring, until the sugar turns a golden brown.

2 Pour the caramel quickly into the large container or divide between the individual ones, tipping so the caramel evenly coats the base and a little way up the sides of the container(s). Leave for a few minutes to set.

3 To make the custard, whisk the eggs together lightly with the sugar, then whisk in the milk and cream and strain into a jug. Whisk the vanilla, allspice and cinnamon into the custard and pour over the caramel.

4 Place the container(s) in a baking tin and add boiling water to come half-way up the sides of the container(s). Lay a sheet of greased greaseproof paper or foil over the custard.

5 Place in a preheated oven at 150°C/300°F/Gas Mark 2, allowing about 45 minutes for the individual custards or 1–1¼ hours for the large one, cooking until set and until a knife inserted in the custard comes out clean. Remove from the water bath and leave to cool; then chill thoroughly.

6 Dip each container briefly in hot water, leave to rest for a minute or so, then shake gently to loosen and invert on to a serving dish or individual plates, allowing the caramel to flow around the custard. Serve plain or with pouring or whipped cream, if liked.

VANILLA & CINNAMON ICE CREAM

This rich creamy ice cream flavoured with vanilla and cinnamon has an added tang from the addition of crème fraîche; chopped toasted nuts can be added. Serve with fresh fruits or a chocolate sauce.

STEP 1

STEP 2

STEP 3

STEP 4

SERVES 4–6

4 eggs
60 g/2 oz caster (superfine) sugar
450 ml /³/₄ pint milk
few drops of vanilla flavouring (extract)
1 tsp ground cinnamon
200 g/7 oz crème fraîche or 300 ml/¹/₂ pint
   double (heavy) cream
45 g/1¹/₂ oz toasted chopped hazelnuts or
   almonds (optional)
fresh fruits to decorate

1 To make the custard, whisk the eggs with the sugar until thick in a heatproof bowl. Heat the milk to just below boiling point and whisk into the egg mixture gradually.

2 Stand the bowl over a pan of gently simmering water and cook gently, stirring almost constantly until thickened sufficiently to coat the back of a spoon quite thickly. Remove from the heat and stir in the vanilla flavouring (extract) and cinnamon. Cover with clingfilm and leave until cold.

3 If using crème fraîche, just mix evenly through the custard; or if using double (heavy) cream, whip until thick but not too stiff and fold into the custard. Cover the bowl or pour into a loaf tin and freeze until just firm.

4 Remove the ice cream from the freezer and whisk until smooth, turning into a bowl if necessary. This breaks down the ice crystals in the ice cream. Beat in the nuts, if using.

5 Cover, return to the freezer and freeze until firm. (An ice cream maker may be used if available.)

6 Serve the ice cream spooned into bowls and decorated with fresh fruits such as strawberries, raspberries, mangoes or guavas; or top with a chocolate sauce.

CHOCOLATE SAUCE

To make the chocolate sauce, melt 125 g/ 4 oz plain chocolate with 30 g/1 oz butter in a bowl and beat in 125 ml/4 fl oz of evaporated milk and a few drops of vanilla flavouring (extract) until smooth, heating a little if necessary to remove any lumps. 1–2 tbsp brandy or rum may also be added.

CHURROS

*Light orange-flavoured fritters, similar to choux puffs, are tossed in
aniseed-flavoured sugar and served hot or cold with a cinnamon syrup.*

STEP 1

STEP 2

STEP 4

STEP 5

SERVES 4–6

60 g/2 oz butter
150 ml/¼ pint water
75 g/2½ oz plain (all-purpose) flour, sifted
2 eggs, beaten
grated rind of ½ orange
oil for deep-frying

ANISEED SUGAR:
5 star anise
90 g/3 oz caster (superfine) sugar

CINNAMON SYRUP:
125 g/4 oz soft brown sugar
150 ml /¼ pint water
2 star anise
½ tsp ground cinnamon
2 tbsp orange juice

1 To make the choux paste, melt the
butter in the water in a saucepan
over a gentle heat; then bring to the boil.
Add the flour all at once, stirring
vigorously over a gentle heat until the
mixture forms a ball, leaving the sides of
the pan clean. Remove from the heat and
leave to cool for 4–5 minutes.

2 To make the aniseed sugar, put the
star anise and sugar into a pestle
and mortar, a food processor or a
blender, and grind until well mixed. Sift
into a bowl.

3 To make the cinnamon syrup, put
the brown sugar into a small pan
with the water, star anise and cinnamon,
and heat until the sugar dissolves; then
boil for about 2 minutes. Stir in the
orange juice and strain into a jug.

4 Add the beaten eggs gradually to
the cooling choux paste, beating
hard (preferably with an electric hand
mixer) until smooth and glossy. The
mixture may not take quite all the egg.
Beat in the orange rind and fill the choux
paste into a large piping bag fitted with a
large star nozzle.

5 Heat the oil to 180°C/350°F or
until a cube of bread browns in
about 1 minute. Pipe 2.5–4 cm/1–1½
inch lengths of the choux paste carefully
into the hot oil, cutting each one off with
a knife, and fry about 6 at a time for
about 3–4 minutes, or until golden
brown and crisp all over.

6 Drain the churros on paper towels,
then toss thoroughly in the aniseed
sugar and serve hot, warm or cold with
the cinnamon syrup.

MEXICAN CUISINE

CHILLIES

As a rough guide, the smaller they are, the hotter they are.

Green chillies are often hotter than red varieties.

The seeds and white veins are the hottest part of all, but have less flavour, so are usually removed before use.

Never put your fingers near your eyes after touching a cut chilli, as they will really burn. Always treat chillies with great care.

Dried chillies are fairly mild in flavour, reddish-brown and well-wrinkled.

Types of chilli
Jalapeño chillies are rich, dark green and hot to very hot, and are also available canned or in a jar. Serrano chillies are small, light green and extremely hot. Mulato, Ancho and Pasilla chillies are all dark brownish-black, rather wrinkled, fruity and slightly sweet with varying degrees of hotness.

Chilli powder
This is made up of ground dried chillies, and often includes ground cumin, salt and a few other spices in small quantities. Each specific make will vary slightly, but it is possible to buy hot, medium and mild varieties of chilli powder. Always add sparingly – it is very powerful.

THE HISTORY OF MEXICAN COOKING

The cuisine of Mexico, though it has changed over the years, remains one that is based on age-old recipes that use the staple foods of the old country – chiefly corn, beans of all kinds, potatoes and sweet potatoes, avocados, tomatoes, chillies, pumpkin, turkey and duck, a wealth of fish from the long coastline, and the delicious cinnamon-flavoured chocolate. Over the centuries, traditional Mexican recipes were combined with the comparatively new influences brought by the conquering Spaniards in the sixteenth century, who arrived with the cattle (for milk and meat), poultry, pigs, wheat, rice, citrus fruits and spices. The combination of the two methods of cooking soon brought forth a wonderful array of new dishes, though they were still based on the old ideas of the Aztecs and Mayans, enhanced with Spanish touches and produce.

SIMPLE RECIPES

Mexican food is easy to prepare at home. With a few exceptions, most of the recipes are uncomplicated and fairly quick to put together. Garnishes and decorations are kept to a minimum, and the food is prepared in a relaxed manner that is reflected in the informal nature of Mexican cuisine. Of course there are certain skills required for a few of the dishes, and the making of the tortilla is probably the most important to master.

Tortillas
The tortilla is really the staple bread of Mexico. Traditionally, it is made with maize flour (masa harina) but can also be made with wheat flour or a combination of the two, which is becoming more popular in the north of the country near to the US border. Maize meal is finely ground corn, pale yellow in colour and available in health-food shops and some supermarkets. It is sometimes called cornmeal but is not the same thing as either polenta or cornflour.

The dough must be properly prepared, rested and then rolled out thickly into a circle, or you can use a tortilla press to make the perfect tortilla. If you have problems rolling the dough into a circle, trim around a suitably sized plate. Tortillas are cooked for the minimum length of time on a heated 'cormal' or heavy-based frying pan, which should be heated slowly and evenly before the tortilla is added; the tortilla is cooked until just speckled brown, then flipped over to cook the second side. If bubbles appear in the surface, they should be pressed down with a rolled-up tea towel or pad of paper towels. The pan should not be greased unless the tortillas stick – normally they do not – and then only lightly with a touch of oil. Once made, wrap in a clean tea towel. If left uncovered, they will immediately firm up. To store them for future use, layer a piece of non-stick baking paper between each tortilla, wrap in a clean tea towel, then put in either a polythene bag or airtight container and chill for up to 3 days. If they become firm they can be reheated in a pan, fried, or dipped briefly in boiling water to soften, so that they can then be further shaped or rolled and used for making other dishes. Tortillas are eaten as a dish in themselves and are also used as the base for a variety of dishes, including Burritos, Tostados, Tacos, Tortilla Chips, Nachos, Enchiladas and Quesadillas.

Chillies

Many people think that all Mexican food is red-hot and almost inedible unless you have a stomach of iron. True, it is highly spiced, and chillies certainly appear in abundance in recipes, but the amount and type of chillies used governs both the spiciness and 'hotness' of the dish, so it is up to the cook to decide just how much or how little to add. There are several types of chilli that are commonly used. However, some of them are readily available only in Mexico and similar countries, so in the recipes I have only stipulated chillis – you can use whichever you prefer or is available.

Beans

Another important ingredient in the Mexican diet is the bean, particularly the pinkish pinto bean, the black bean and the red kidney bean. Both fresh and dried beans are used widely to serve as 'stewed' or 'pot' beans as an everyday dish. Long, slow cooking is essential to make the beans digestible, and salt should be added only when they are tender, or the beans will take forever to tenderize. Many flavours can be added during cooking, including onions, chillies, bacon, garlic, and many others, which the beans readily absorb.

Each type of bean has its own special quality and flavour, and every family will have its own particular way of cooking them, either to be eaten as they are, or to be turned into Refried Beans. This is another traditional (and famous) Mexican dish, which can be eaten as a dish in its own right, or it can form part of many other Mexican dishes, particularly in combination with tortillas and their various fillings and toppings. Stewed or pot beans (or drained canned beans) are added to fried onion, garlic and chilli, mashed as they are added and then cooked to a thick paste to serve either hot or cold.

Salads

Guacamole and Tomato Salsa are regular accompaniments to many Mexican dishes, and are flavoured with chillies and onions; they are very attractive and tasty and can be eaten alone as well as being presented as a side dish to other foods. Other salads tend to use a mixture of fruit and vegetables, often combining flavours we may not be used to, but which turn out to blend extremely well. For instance, beetroot, bananas, mangoes and pomegranates are often mixed with a range of vegetables, giving the finished dish colour, texture and an original flavour.

Peppers

Peppers feature extensively in Mexican cookery, in all varieties and colours, including red, green, orange and yellow.

OTHER INGREDIENTS

Cheese in Mexican cooking

Use a white crumbly cheese such as Wensleydale, Cheshire, Lancashire or Greek Feta as the best substitutes for the salty Mexican cheeses; or a mixture of Cheddar and Mozzarella.

Cooking fats

Good pork lard is most widely used in Mexico in cooking, but vegetable oils and butter make good substitutes.

Cream

Cream in Mexico is similar to the French crème fraîche, but is often difficult to find. To make your own, add 1 tbspn of natural yogurt to 300 ml/½ pint whipping cream and leave overnight, or add 2 tspns buttermilk to 450 ml/¾ pint double cream and leave at room temperature for up to 24 hours until thickened, and then refrigerate. Alternatively, use soured cream.

Tomatoes

In Mexico, tomatoes grow large and unevenly shaped, similar to beefsteak or Mediterranean varieties. For the most authentic Mexican shaped and flavoured tomatoes, use those sun ripened in the garden, not grown in a greenhouse.

Star anise

This is the dried star-shaped fruit of an evergreen tree with a strong aniseed flavour.

USING A TORTILLA PRESS

These are available from specialist kitchen equipment shops and larger department stores. They ensure evenly shaped and thin tortillas all of a regular size, something that takes time and a lot of practice to achieve by hand.

Line the base of the press with a square of greaseproof, non-stick baking paper. Flatten a piece of tortilla dough about the size of a small egg, then place on the paper and cover with another piece of paper. Close the press, pushing down the handle firmly.

Open the press, remove the top piece of paper and invert the tortilla on to a hot griddle, or stack up between damp cloths, or put into an airtight container until ready to cook.

HANDY TIP

Enriching stews
To enrich an already well flavoured and rich meat stew or casserole, add 25–40g/1–1½ oz Mexican chocolate or plain dark chocolate and a pinch of ground cinnamon, stirring until well melted and absorbed into the juices.

Some people find the taste of pepper can be harsh and almost bitter. To remove this, the Mexicans always roast or toast the pepper to peel the skin, which in turn takes away any bitterness. It is simple to do. First cut the pepper in half from stem to tip and lay the pieces cut-side down on a foil-lined grill rack and cook under a moderate heat until the skin chars and turns completely black. Remove and leave to cool a little and then the skin will peel off easily. Finally, turn over the pepper and remove the stem, membrane and any seeds and it is ready for use. Peppers may also be dry-fried by placing each half skin-side down in a 'cormal' or heavy-based frying pan and cooked slowly over a low heat until the skin blisters and chars.

Tomatoes

Tomatoes are an important part of Mexican cuisine, as they are used in salads – including the indispensable Tomato Salsa – as well as in a great many main-course dishes and a wide range of sauces. If they are to be cooked or added to cooked dishes, the skins are always removed first. This can be done in either of two ways. One is to place the tomatoes in a bowl and cover them with boiling water for a minute, then make a nick in the skin with a knife and transfer them quickly to a bowl of cold water. The skin will then peel off easily. Another method, if you have a gas hob, is to impale the tomato on a long fork and hold it carefully over the flame, turning it so that it heats evenly, until the skin chars and splits, after which it will peel off easily. This can also be done by

placing the tomato under a hot grill until the skin just chars and splits.

Coriander (cilantro)

Also known as Chinese parsley, coriander (cilantro) is used in many Mexican recipes, either as a flavouring ingredient or as a garnish. It has a fairly potent but refreshing flavour, and is a true taste of Mexico. However, it does wilt extremely easily, so should be picked fresh or kept in cold water.

Coriander seeds and ground coriander are also used in Mexican cuisine, but the flavours are quite different, and fresh coriander (cilantro) and seed coriander are not interchangeable.

Spices

Several spices feature frequently in Mexican recipes, particularly cumin and cinnamon. Cumin, either in seed or powdered form, gives a touch of the oriental flavour brought by Indian settlers; cinnamon, used both ground and in stick form, is found in both sweet and savoury dishes. Mexican chocolate is flavoured with cinnamon also, and if you use any other type of chocolate for a Mexican recipe, it is advisable to add a pinch of ground cinnamon for an authentic taste. Cloves too are used frequently in Mexican dishes, often in their ground form.

Pumpkin seeds

When the skin is removed from pumpkin seeds, the familiar green seeds are revealed, which are known as 'pepitas'. They can be added to dishes as they are, or they can be toasted or roasted first.

Often ground up to make a dip or dressing, they have a delicious nutty flavour and are extremely nutritious. If you cannot find them in your local supermarket, they are usually available from health-food shops.

Tacos

These can be bought ready-made in airtight packets and are often eaten as a snack – the Mexican version of potato crisps. They can easily be made at home simply by cutting homemade tortillas into wedges and frying them in deep or shallow fat until they are crispy. They are ideal for serving with dips such as Guacamole, as the dips complement the dry hot taste of the tacos. Once fried, they can be kept for up to a week in an airtight container.

Mexican drinks

There are several drinks associated with Mexico, most of which are pretty, and ideal for a party. Everyone knows the famous Tequila Sunrise – a mixture of tequila, orange juice, a touch of grenadine and lime juice, served with crushed ice. The Margarita is perhaps equally famous; it is a blend of tequila, lime juice, clear orange liqueur such as Cointreau and crushed ice.

Every country has its own version of fresh lemonade and in Mexico it is particularly refreshing; but whether or not you ever visit Mexico and try the lemonade, you must sample their hot chocolate. Put 750ml/1¼ pints of milk into a saucepan with 3 thin strips of orange rind, bring barely to the boil, remove from the heat, cover and leave to stand for 5 minutes; then discard the rind. Blend 90g/3½ oz Mexican chocolate or plain dark chocolate with a good pinch of ground cinnamon with the milk until dissolved and whisk until the mixture is really frothy. Serve at once, topped with a pinch of ground cinnamon – quite delicious!

Freezing

On the whole, Mexican food is not very suitable for freezing, mainly because of the strong flavours involved – particularly chillies and chilli sauces, which are widely used. When strong flavours are frozen they tend to intensify, and if left for more than a couple of weeks, a musty flavour can develop which spoils the dish, although it is not harmful. So before you decide to freeze a dish, consider whether it is really going to be helpful, and do so only if necessary and then for just a couple of weeks or so. Tortillas, which are widely used in the Mexican diet, cannot be frozen, so this does make many of the recipes unsuitable for freezing as they feature in them so frequently.

Mexican food is very distinctive, but with its simplicity and the wide use of fresh local produce you will find, as many people do, that the flavours and spiciness can quickly become almost addictive. Whether you want to serve a complete Mexican meal, or intersperse your cooking with a starter, main dish or dessert with a Mexican flavour, or just serve one of the delicious snacks, you are sure to be pleasantly surprised by the simplicity of the preparation and the mouth-watering results.

SALSA VERDE

An alternative to tomato salsa (see page 24), this salad makes an attractive and different accompaniment to Mexican dishes.

*500g/1lb tomatillos or green
  tomatoes, chopped*
*½ medium onion, chopped very
  finely*
*1 level tbsp fresh coriander
  (cilantro), chopped*
salt and pepper

Mix well, turn into a bowl and cover with clingfilm (plastic food wrap). Chill for at least 30 minutes.

MEXICAN SALAD DRESSING

*6 tbsps sunflower oil, or olive oil,
  or a mixture of the two*
2 tbsps white wine vinegar
½ level tsp Dijon mustard
pinch granulated sugar
*1–2 level tbsps fresh coriander
  (cilantro), chopped*
salt and pepper

1. Put all the ingredients into a screw-top jar. Shake thoroughly until emulsified.

2. Store for 3–4 days in the refrigerator.

3. Without the addition of the fresh coriander (cilantro), the dressing will keep for up to 10 days – just add the herb before serving.

INDEX